Words Vividly Shared

Raymond L. Stewart

AKA

"Twilight"

Produced by Aspen Tree Ministries.

DEDICATION

The following pages are dedicated to Ms. Wendy Lippard, who increased my boundary of understanding beyond any measure.

Ms. Lippard visited a prison in Tennessee to facilitate the End Violence Workshop. End Violence is a leadership and transformational thinking workshop. Through her ability to VIVIDLY SHARE, my life was enriched.

We believe that life is a puzzle, and people are the pieces of that puzzle. Without all the pieces, I would have never completed my puzzle. Because of her willingness to come into a maximum security prison and show love, I have value.

Ms. Lippard gave me HER strength, HER boldness in speech, HER love, but mostly SHE gave me the ability to assertively listen to all. I pray to have HER ability of sharing vividly. Thanks, Wendy, for making this puzzle clear and almost complete through your empowering conversation.

Much Love

Raymond L. Stewart

AKA

"Twilight"

T W I LIGHT
O A N
L
K

Twilight... To Walk In Light

I

Acknowledgements

My Family   for Believing in Me

Men of Journey   for Accountability

End Violence for Wendy Lippard

Western Kentucky   for Dr. Kate King

Think Tank   for Love of Humanity

Special Needs Prison for the Kind Staff

Aspen Tree Ministries for Reverend Diana DeWitt

We Stay Free   for Ms. D. And Mr. E. Truitt

Law of Goodness   for Janice Denton, Photographs

Law of Attraction   for Dr. Audrey L. Anton

Law of Peace for Nancy and Hank Miles, Editing

GOD   FOR ALL MENTIONED AND THE CONTENTS OF
THIS BOOK

"TO GOD BE THE GLORY"

v

Contents

Introduction

This book of poems will bring you along with me from 1987 to the present, where the positive change is tangibly clear through my early writings until now.

You will clearly see the brokenness and darkness in my early writings. You will also see the repaired love and light in my present writings. Darkness is the absence of light, where love is an intense affectionate concern for another person.

Through empowering conversations with other people, I KNOW I LOVE HUMANITY.

"GOD IS"

Words Vividly Shared

VIRTUES

What's up with everybody, seven tears dropped.
A full cycle has been completed; pain heals,
but hurt is never forgotten.

Wicked-minded people boast about all kinds of stuff,
but the righteous at heart will be humble
until pushed too far.

A warrior dies only once, but a coward dies continually.
To be true to yourself brings truth.

To abuse righteousness is the equivalent of
a righteous man losing his mind.

A righteous man is forthright and up-front,
with righteous virtues as his backbone.

He will be part and parcel of God Himself.
Man must trust his maker's will
for good virtues to flourish.

Your humble servant,
Twilight
September 16, 1987

UNFOLDED

I saw who I was.
Very unpleasant.

I see who I am,
Forgiven by Grace and Mercy.

I've seen where I'll spend eternity,
Through the Word of God.

"Live in your Vision,
and you shall always be Happy!"

Your humble servant,
Twilight

Trapped In Me

I often feel as if I'm putting my foot in my mouth. Always in some kind of conflict or turmoil, I'm being worn down to DUST. What can I do? My nature is aggression, my purpose is to destroy, but my actions are unpredictable. I need stability. This is my promise to peace, my vow to God and myself:

Lord, please make all my desires, your desires; let me show and guide you God in the right direction, with pure peace and peace of mind. My mind.

Twilight
Zone
December 17, 1987

OUR CHOICE

In life, what sometimes appears to be the end
could be a beginning!

The beginning of something new,
you decide if good or bad.

"Live in your Vision,
and you shall always be Happy!"

Your humble servant,
Twilight

ME, MYSELF, AND I

I had not felt these feelings
of shame and pain for many years.

You have all that you need, but I want
you to have all that you want.

My mind might be primitive,
but you deserve it all. I'm partial.

I really don't know if it's the
sight of you, why I love you so much.

With all the evil you've done,
looking at you sometimes is hard.

If I could stop seeing you above others,
I could see equal value in us all.

It's strength that I need
to see love for more than myself.

So I'll stay out of the mirror
and see a collective love for mankind.

Your humble servant,
Twilight

MANIFEST

All of our dreams shall come true,
when we gain the strength to follow them.

"Live in your Vision,
and you shall always be Happy!"

Your humble servant,
Twilight

MANHOOD

I'm falling deeper and deeper in despair.
I'm trying so hard to focus, to stay on the straight path,
to be positive, to pray for patience.
And it seems all to be a fruitless effort.

I'm crying on paper I know,
but I need to release this in a constructive manner.
Love is pain, concern equals up to letdowns and defeat.
Being positive seems to be meaningless.

This confusion I harbor has depth
and is utterly consuming.
My better nature of morals, principles, and values
all at this point seem outdated.

It's most plain to see, I'm feeling sorry for myself.
But still, I'm looking for peace
and freedom in the spiritual.
It is ordained by GOD, so it shall be.

Your humble servant,
Twilight

INVESTMENT

Invest in the well-being of someone else,
with love as your profit.

Then watch your investment grow.

"Live in your Vision,
and you shall always be Happy!"

Your humble servant,
Twilight

HURT

Downward spiral, deeply unmoved by falseness,
so tired of surface talk.
I'm of a spiritual nature, so I shun my contempt
for those who can't be honest in themselves.

It hurts to have depth but unmovable interest,
for I can be inspired by the smallest things,
such as an image or phrase.
It's equally hurtful to know myself,
but get deceived by this pumping muscle
inside my rib cage.

For this I'm in a constant state
of confusion and bewilderment.
My better judgment is always
having a conflict of interest with my heart.

Downward slipping into a depth unknown.
Who is here and where shall I go,
Desperate to make a connection,
but reluctant to love.

For this reason, my biggest life lesson thus far is
LOVE IS PAIN.

Your humble servant,
Twilight

TRUTH

God recognizes you, and Satan recognizes you,
But do you recognize you?

If you truly and truthfully look at yourself,
and see the true you,

Then you shall know who you belong to.
God or Satan?

"Live in your Vision,
and you shall always be Happy!"

Your humble servant,
Twilight

WHY

Born to struggle,
moving around the world without direction.
Why?

Born to struggle,
moving around the world without protection.
Why?

Born to struggle, moving around the world,
only a body without a mind.
Why?

Born to struggle, in love with the hope of bliss,
yet that notion dismissed.
Why?

Born to struggle, child of the dust,
"we" must trust there is a purpose in pondering.
Why?

Born to struggle, we must believe in the power
to achieve happiness and peace.
Why?

Life is a struggle, to stop is to die.
That's why I'm no longer able to ask
"Why."

Your humble servant,
Twilight

BEHAVE

Love is not a feeling,

It's a behavior
filled with actions of care.

Love is clear to see.

"Live in your Vision,
and you shall always be Happy!"

Your humble servant,
Twilight

EVERYDAY

Everyday I pray to be the center of your life.

Everyday I'm not.

Everyday I wake up with good intentions,
but through the day they turn bitter.

Everyday I hear people talk crazy
about the ones who love them.

Everyday I lose faith in the people who knew me,
but now are only images in my mind.

Everyday I fight inner demons.

Everyday I learn more about the world I live in.

Everyday I feel so numb, less like me and more like YOU.

YOU, the world that lessoned me with hatred,
and clothed me with rage.

Everyday I pray for release from my confines.

Everyday I pray for love, and to be thought of.

Everyday I pray to be the center of your life.

And everyday I'm not.

Your humble servant,
Twilight

FIRST LAW

Self-preservation is the first law of nature,
animal instinct.

Love your brother is the first law of God's children,
CHRIST instinct.

"Live in your Vision,
and you shall always be Happy!"

Your humble servant,
Twilight

AWARENESS

Self-awareness is an untouchable force
because you can't put a limit on its boundaries.

That's like trying to measure the universe with a ruler!
The mind's only limit is the one you put on it.

Be mindful of the people you influence
through words, acts, deeds, and above all, be truthful;

Truthful to yourself or every person you come in contact with
will be an object opposed to a friend.

Don't use intellect as a weapon of destruction,
use higher thought as a bridge for peace with yourself,
then pass that insight on to the others.

Simplicity is the easiest way to be,
but first you need to be honest and truthful to self.

See, it always comes back to who you are to yourself.
Let the sight of yourself be pure and clean.
Then and only then have you made society better.

Your humble servant,
Twilight

BE RIGHT

When you believe you can,
you will.

When you don't believe you can,
you won't.

However you believe,
it will be true.

I believe I'll serve God forever.

"Live in your Vision,
and you shall always be Happy!"

Your humble servant,
Twilight

WAR

I now attempt to spit my conflict within
on this body of paper.
Have mercy on me.

To have her or to have her not!
This is my prolonged mental fight.
Have mercy on me.

She belongs to another.
To have her I know would be wrong.
I don't want to be right.
Have mercy on me.

To see the love for Christ in her eyes,
we know in our hearts we have to resist.
Have mercy on us.

When it's all said and done,
we know that in life and in death,
We belong to GOD.
He has mercy on us.

Your humble servant,
Twilight

INVISIBLE

You see me so clearly, and know I'm real.
I really can't see myself; I'm invisible.

You see my strength and proud look.
I hear my thoughts, my doubt is clear.

You see what I could be, my future bright.
I know my past has control of my present.

You see my focus and attention to detail.
I see the end result, my focus is cloudy.

You see my vision I shared so vividly.
I know it's the collective
that brings the vision to life.

We know it's not you or me,
but the FAITH of the collective
that will make LOVE clear.

Your humble servant,
Twilight

DELIGHT

I just got off work, from doing my duty.
Decided to fly you a kite, for my delight.

It's not sympathy, why I fly this kite,
It's all empathy, why I pray for you at night.

Though this season has brought you
sorrow and pain,
In your vision I walk, our pain the same.

You've given me much, value to me the devil,
In the circle we trust, all people same level.

While our days be long, the connection still strong,
I'm your humble seed, to help in time of need.

To say I'm committed to taking your pain,
something pretty to say,
while I feel helplessly insane.

So I'll simply say

I love you.

Your humble servant
Twilight

TEMPLE

The word teaches us
that we are the temples of God.
If anyone defile the temple,
God shall destroy.
Why do we defile the temple
that God made us caretakers of?

"Live in your Vision,
and you shall always be Happy!"

Your humble servant,
Twilight

WINNIE KATE

I really don't remember when I returned.

I really don't know if I'm back.

I really don't know when I left.

I really don't know why I left.

I really don't know how I got there.

I really don't know how I fell out of love with life.

I really don't think life is fair.

I really don't know what life is.

Perhaps, it's to be kind!

Kind to myself, also.

Your humble servant,
Twilight

KINGDOM

In the presence of God
we won't compete or hate.
Remember, we are ALWAYS
in the presence of God.

"Live in your Vision,
and you shall always be Happy!"

Your humble servant,
Twilight

VORTEX

It's a cold March dawn,
with my chore of emptying trash at hand.

I take a second to gaze upon the snowcap hills
through the eyes of many years.

I remembered my youth and amazement of God,
who to my delight had made such a beautiful sight.

While I continue to gaze into the past,
I realize the snowcap hills
have become invisible for many years.

Through my desire to have the things made by man,
I lost sight of the wonders provided by God's hand.

I remembered the trash and the chore to be done.
It caused one last look upon the beauty at hand.

A quick peak at my watch before completing the chore,
the vortex over my present beautiful, my past my past.

Your humble servant,
Twilight

CONVERSATION

Please God,
I don't want to do anything wrong.
Help me to KNOW you,
and to KNOW the right way.

Thank you, Father.

"Live in your Vision,
and you shall always be Happy!"

Your humble servant,
Twilight

ONE REASON

I really didn't like or love you
for these many reasons:

You were selfish, self-centered, unconcerned,
bitter, without spirit or feelings.

You were evil and unalive, a shell of a person.
I cursed the day you were born.

You didn't have hope,
you were driven by desires outside your reach,
and blinded by your ignorance.

By God's grace and mercy,
I now like and love myself for one reason,

God made me in His image and likeness.
In this I walk.

Your humble servant
Twilight

STARTING POINT

Don't watch the preacher,
because he might let you down.

Watch God only.

Don't compare yourself to others.
Compare yourself to who you WERE yesterday!

"Live in your Vision,
and you shall always be Happy!"

Your humble servant,
Twilight

YESTERYEARS

My mind is wondering about God and my purpose,
I'm angry, frustrated,
and my pen is spitting venom on this body of paper....
but still I struggle.

Scattered thoughts, misplaced memories of love,
feels like a long, outdated precious moment.
God, where are you?

I feel like I have the right to request your presence,
however, I realize your presence is all around.

I have so many resentments, so many questions,
but don't have no beginning, but I feel the end is near.

That depression turns to anger, then rage,
and I'm afraid of the next logical step,
Death....Should I be afraid of the inescapable?

I love life, regardless of the obstacles in my path.
It's my views I'm struggling with.
God, please present yourself and show me my purpose.

My mind, heart, and spirit seek and thirst for you, Father.
Why can't I manage to find you?
Please show me your path, and I'll follow.

Your humble servant,
Twilight

PREDICTION

I see a world filled with love and peace.

A world where love and peace
are the foundation of this creation.

"Live in your Vision,
and you shall always be Happy!"

Your humble servant,
Twilight

OUR MOMENT

So many images in my mind that
I would love to remove, the devil I was.

I saw you today, my mind skipped a thought,
So pleasantly real, the devil I was.

The image of you has consumed my thoughts!
So warm they heal, the devil I was.

Today almost gone and tomorrow soon to come,
Infinity will be ours, the devil I was.

The glance in your eyes has captured my soul,
My dream a reality, the devil I was.

Belonging to you has given me value,
Complete because of you, the devil I was.

You anchor my spirit to a profound fact,
That in life and in death, we belong to God.
We belong to GOD.

Your humble servant,
Twilight

INSANITY

Wisdom is the application of knowledge.

To continue sinning, once you know
that the wages of sin is death,
makes you unwise.

"Live in your Vision,
and you shall always be Happy!"

Your humble servant,
Twilight

CLARITY

As I empty myself on this body of paper,
my mind takes flight,
far, far away from my current state,

Soaring in the windstream of the northern coast,
I'm floating, amazed at the wonders
of my Father's creation
of land, sea, and man.

Mesmerized by the clarity of the world from high above,
I'm alone in this journey, yet I feel like
I'm in a flock, I'm protected by knowing
my flight is by God's beautiful grace,
and His presence keeps me afloat.

Crossing the countryside, eager to rest,
but I'm not in control,
My Father knows best, he created all,
and thought me into existence.

It's amazing to witness My Father's grace,
the beauty of it all.
Anyone can have my place.
This journey has given me the power of love,
the kind of love that shows.

Your humble servant,
Twilight

FOR ME

It's better to love God
and have no friends,
than to have lots of friends,
and have no God.

"Live in your Vision,
and you shall always be Happy!"

Your humble servant,
Twilight

MIND GALLERY

I am blessed with the most expensive
art gallery in the universe.

Four halls with paintings and photographs
on both sides of the walls.

The appearance of all the art different,
but the expression tells the same story,

An expression of peace, hope, joy, and love,
the warm essence of her image floods the halls.

Eight walls of precious art to be adored,
because one touch would destroy the moment.

The four halls of my mind, the art gallery just fine,
always divine, and all mine.

Your humble servant,
Twilight

DOUBLE TALK

You say you have the spirit,
and live in the spirit,
yet you walk in darkness.

Your talk is untrue,
and your Father is evident.

"Live in your Vision,
and you shall always be Happy!"

Your humble servant,
Twilight

TESTIMONY

My brother communicated his concern for my soul.
Darkness on bodies of paper, created by my mind,

I never imagined monsters were real.
Face the cruel anger of man, see how you feel.

The scars healed, but the pain stained my mind,
That same stain gave me the right to destroy.

I'll rule in hell, never serve in heaven.
Mother will tell how she prayed for the living.

I no longer wonder why I wandered in darkness,
Consumed by shame and fear,
driven by the need of respect.

I don't deserve anything, something pretty to say,
I can't forgive myself, just a play on words.

JESUS died on the cross, to redeem my soul,
GOD's grace and mercy has made me whole.

So I'll write in the light, for my brother's delight,
And I'll walk in love, by my Father's might.

Your humble servant,
Twilight

THE SIXTH SENSE

I was able to TOUCH, but was
unable to feel love or others.

I was able to TASTE, but was
unable to get full, because of gluttony.

I was able to SMELL, but was
unable to catch the scent of my stinky behavior.

I was able to HEAR, but was
unable to perceive that my tongue knew no shame.

I was able to SEE, but was
unable to focus my eyes on the monster I was.

Then you came, and opened my mind,
I thought I had sanity, but was full of insanity.
Now that you are my active force, I am sane.

You are the Alpha and Omega,
You are I AM, my Sixth Sense.

Your humble servant,
Twilight

MY LIGHTHOUSE

Bad seed I was, with
Bad deeds my claim to fame.

The depths of my mind,
darker than Mammoth Cave,
No light or flame.

She entered my world with a new conversation,
So bright, my darkness she tamed.

Beautiful she is,
but it's her wisdom and passion for humanity,
Why I speak her name.

The fame unclaimed, no flame! That's insane.
The darkness tamed, her name shall remain.

Thanks for illuminating,
This once dark Mammoth Cave.

Your humble servant,
Twilight

GOD'S CHILDREN

I proudly served Satan with my life,
as I walked a wicked path.

Imprisoned for many, many bad deeds,
where I've been saved by God's seeds.

God's servants illuminated my spirit,
with a guiding light of hope, so deeply rooted.

For a profound fact, it's through my captivity
that my soul has been saved.

Through faith of God's children, now I'm found,
but once I was lost.

Your humble servant,
Twilight

PREPARE

The scriptures teach us,
that the only offensive weapon
needed to defeat Satan
is the Word of God.

Learn the Word,
and stay prepared for the war.

"Live in your Vision,
and you shall always be Happy!"

Your humble servant,
Twilight

DUEL

"They had" is temporal
and speaks of memories of pleasure,
driven by pleasure.

"We have" is continual
and speaks of memories of love,
driven by love.

They had the world and all it could offer
to please the flesh for a season.

We have the Father
and all the connections of his children,
to share love is the reason.

They had the same promise,
but through disobedience
are separated for eternity

We have the love, for loving our way back to God,
and be in his presence for infinity.

Your humble servant,
Twilight

ALWAYS

Don't think about the evil
that tomorrow could bring,

because tomorrow shall always be there.

Focus on overcoming the evil TODAY!

"Live in your Vision,
and you shall always be Happy!"

Your humble servant,
Twilight

SERVANT

They called me Sinner,
because I committed many offenses
and violations against God.

They call me Messenger,
because I'm charged
with spreading the word of God.

They call me Disciple,
because I believe in God
and help spread the teachings of God.

They call me Apostle;
they say I'm divinely called and sent forth by God.

I call myself a servant of the most high God,
who speaks submission to God.

In the past I forgot that in life and in death,
I belong to God.
Thank you, Father.

Your humble servant,
Twilight

GOD'S PLAN

It's the time between the past and future.
It's brief; it's a split second.

It's all that's real, and
It's where your POWER lies.

Use it to serve God
and become immortal.

"Live in your Vision,
and you shall always be Happy!"

Your humble servant,
Twilight

GOD IS

Yesterday I thought that God, the Bible, and Jesus
were only figments of some author's imagination.

Today, I know that GOD, the Bible,
and Jesus are real.
GOD is our Father, the Bible is our Instructions,
and Jesus is our Savior.

Tomorrow I'll be in the presence of GOD,
not because of anything I've done.
I'm a sinner saved by grace.

I've said it before, and I'll say it again:
Jesus died on the cross to redeem my soul.

GOD's grace and mercy has made me whole.

Your humble servant,
Twilight

FORGIVENESS

After being crucified at Calvary,

He said,
"Father, forgive them,
for they know not what they do."

I can only say,
"Thank you, Father, for your forgiveness."

"Live in your Vision,
and you shall always be Happy!"

Your humble servant,
Twilight

TRANSCEND

Mother! The light of her spirit, unknown,
unnoticed and unloved by her sibling or father.

She smiles as she peeks into the future,
where nothing is visible

She frowns as she glances into the past,
where displeasure haunts her.

She's illuminated in my presence as she
remembers her mother's spirit in the hot breeze.

Held so tenderly by the cool air of the hot breeze,
as only a mother could.

She rises above life as she comes to realize
GOD IS.

Your humble servant,
Twilight

ONE ROAD

The road of exclusion leads nowhere
but a dead end of death.

The road of inclusion is the Golden Rule
of all religious scriptures
that leads to ETERNAL LIFE.

"Live in your Vision,
and you shall always be Happy!"

Your humble servant,
Twilight

FAMILY

Created in our Father's image,
Raised in our Father's business.

Our Father's business is people.
Now we address you, wonderful person.

It's not by duty that we share these words,
Only our delight to make your days bright.

It's our Father's vision, "Love one another."
Words are nothing without deeds and action.

In our deeds and actions, his vision is clear:
We walk in the light, to God be the glory.

Only a servant of the most high God
Will always take pleasure in doing His will.

Rest...mental or emotional serenity.
May the spirit of peace and rest,
rule and abide with us now and forever.

We ask only that you would consider this new
conversation.

Your humble servant,
Twilight

SUPPORT

After a student comes to know God,
the Battle really starts.

The Teacher must be there, because Satan is,
and the Battle is constant.

So our Walk must be constant, also.

"Live in your Vision,
and you shall always be Happy!"

Your humble servant,
Twilight

DEPRESSED

I slept within my sleep
and dreamed within my dream.
The longer I slept, the more intoxicated I became.

Blinded by anger and consumed with rage,
but unable to awake,
I hear a knock at the door
from deep within my mind.

Aware, but unaware,
that the displeasure of the moment
was destroying the vision of my future.
After ten minutes, I rise from the pit of my dreams.

I open the door, but no one is there,
so I begin to stare into the cool night air,
when the voice of peace speaks:

Close the door, and just let go,
and then you will know!
GOD IS!

Your humble servant,
Twilight

BEAUTY

Dream love!

Because the future belongs
to those who believe
in the beauty of their dreams.

"Live in your Vision,
and you shall always be Happy!"

Your humble servant,
Twilight

I AM

It has been said over and over again by people all over the world, by men and women, old and young:

"I love you from the bottom of my heart."

"I always have and I always will."

"I loved you from first sight."

Only God knows who said it first or who will say it last, but you can rest assured, it will be said again.

So, I'll simply say it like this:

I love you from the center of my being, because you are my center.

Without you, I was only a being, driven by seeds of wickedness that drove me to deeds of wickedness. Then you came and took control of the center of my being to rest, rule, and abide. You are my guide to the path of righteousness.

You are my center.

You are I AM.

Your humble servant,

Twilight

SHAPE

We are formed and educated by what we love.

Let GOD be the center of your love.

And your light shall shine.

"Live in your Vision,
and you shall always be Happy!"

Your humble servant,
Twilight

CHERISH

I envision the perfect woman,
the woman in which I could cherish.

I want to be the perfect man,
the man in which she could cherish.

Her perfection is clear
as she shares the love of God,
her spirit flourishes.

My perfection is near
because of the kindness she shared,
my spirit is nourished.

By God's grace, we are nourished.
By God's mercy, we shall flourish.

By God's gift, we have perfection,
so it's God we cherish.

"Live in your Vision,
and you shall always be Happy!"

Your humble servant,
Twilight

LAST HOUR

It has been said for centuries upon centuries,
all over the planet,

Mankind for certain is the only part of creation
that knows it has to die.

Even a more profound thought -
to only have one hour of life left. Wow!

That hour has been spent in so many ways,
nobody wrong, their hour their own.

For an absolute fact, it's with my soul mate
that my last hour would be spent.

It's not because of her beauty, but beautiful she is,
and that's a matter of fact.

In her presence is the closest I've ever felt to GOD.

So to spend my last hour sleeping in her arms,
would be a beautiful thing.

Your humble servant,
Twilight

NOW

The past was mine,
where I loved only myself
and couldn't imagine a world without me in it.

The present is yours,
where I love only you
and can't imagine a world without you in it.

The future will be ours,
where we will love only one another,
and won't imagine a world without the other in it.

The past, present and future are all one:
the past gone, the present at hand, and
the future uncertain.

Should I tell you how I feel?
Should I?

Your humble servant,
Twilight

THE WORD

In life, when you divide the people,
it's easy to conquer them.

In spiritualism, walking in LOVE
conquers death.

"Live in your Vision,
and you shall always be Happy!"

Your humble servant,
Twilight

DISPLACED

Not too long ago, when I laid down at night,
I could hear the grass grow.

After sunrise, I would watch the wind blow the grass
I heard grow the night before.

Displaced by force, by the dark and lost,
to a strange wasteland of their choice.

I was no longer able to hear the grass grow,
and unable to see the wind blow.

I now realize, it's my inner peace that allows me
to hear the grass grow, and see the wind blow.

Circumstances, situations, and locations are temporal,
where inner peace comes from the presence of God.

I hear the grass grow and see the wind blow.

Your humble servant,
Twilight

PRAISE GOD

The purpose of life is to live a life of purpose!

Our purpose is to praise GOD and let love be seen.

"Live in your Vision,
and you shall always be Happy!"

Your humble servant,
Twilight

WITNESS

You speak of the goodness that you see within me.

I walk by the goodness of the thoughts
of his children within me.

What you see is the grace of our Father,
his love is clear.

What I feel is the mercy of our father,
his forgiveness is near.

By the word of God we know!

The spirit itself beareth witness with our spirit
that we are the children of God.

Your humble servant,
Twilight

SUCCESS

If knowledge is truly the key to success,
then to KNOW GOD
is the key to ETERNAL SUCCESS.

"Live in your Vision,
and you shall always be Happy!"

Your humble servant,
Twilight

LAST STAR

When I was a child
we would gaze at the stars all hours of night.
Wow, what a beautiful sight!

One by one,
we would count them and wonder how many it was.
Wow, what a beautiful sight!

On really bright nights, we would watch the wind blow.
Wow, what a beautiful sight!

On clear, rainy nights, with the stars still bright,
we would watch the rain dance on the ocean.
Wow, what a beautiful sight!

To watch the stars
cause the mountains to cast a shadow ten miles long,
Wow, what a beautiful sight!

As the years pass and the stars begin to fall without notice,
Wow, what a beautiful sight!

On May 25, 2014, the last star fell, and we all noticed,
the last beautiful sight gone.

To our surprise, the thought of Lucille, the last star,
and the memories of how beautiful she made the ocean,
mountains, and wind appear free,
Wow, what a beautiful thought!

Your humble servant
Twilight

RIGHT NOW

"I don't know"
is the beginning of everything.

To know that you don't know
is profound and rewarding.

Know this!
Tomorrow never comes.
All that is real is now,
Right now.

So serve God,
and spend eternity in His presence.

"Live in your Vision,
and you shall always be Happy!"

Your humble servant,
Twilight

SOUL MATE

The sight of the sunrise outside my window,
warms my soul.

The thoughts of your smile inside my mind,
warms my spirit.

You being outside my presence is pain,
that words won't describe.

You being inside my memories is joy,
that words can't describe.

Inside or outside, it's the knowledge of God's love
for his humble servant that lets me know,
one day I'll see your smile as the sunrise.

Because GOD IS.

Your humble servant,
Twilight

DECISION

When you decide to forgive,
You shall be lifted to a height beyond Belief.
But if you decide to hold Hate,
You shall be crippled for Life.

"Live in your Vision,
and you shall always be Happy!"

Your humble servant,
Twilight

"SIX WORD MEMOIR"
PAIN
MANY PAINFUL IMAGES!
HELP ME FORGET.

The blank stare on your face
and dead look in your eyes
reveal the hurt of your thoughts.

Your thoughts are real,
to forget would be a shame.

The shame belongs to the one
who caused you so much pain.

Your pain is a conversation,
to be shouted to the world and beyond.

This conversation shouted will heal your spirit,
giving the peace you've longed for.

Your humble servant,
Twilight

JESUS

By God's Divine Grace and Mercy,
What he has given me,
Was built upon the STONE
The builders refused.

God's plan is perfect
and his Will,
will be.

"Live in your Vision,
and you shall always be Happy!"

Your humble servant,
Twilight

HONESTY

Things are created,
then mailed all around the world
with instructions: Fragile, handle with care.

Created by your parents,
sent into a land full of dishonesty,
without instructions, you couldn't bear.

You're a woman; you feel like a child,
lost in a jungle filled with deception
and no truthfulness.

You wonder, am I on another planet, or is
my mind playing tricks on me? No love or trust.

Your heart is pure,
you only pray to see goodness in mankind;
an angel you are.

Here are your instructions:
Fragile, handle with care.
I BELONG TO GOD.

Your humble servant
Twilight

SANCTUARY

It has been said,
"Home is where the heart is."

Where is your heart?
Heaven, I pray.

"Live in your Vision,
and you shall always be Happy!"

Your humble servant,
Twilight

LOVE

In our minds, we are incomplete.
In our minds, we daydream.

In your eyes, I see your pain.
In my eyes, you see hope.

In your presence, I feel joy.
In my presence, you feel safe.

In your eyes, I see your thoughts.
In my eyes, your hear my thoughts.

In your arms, I see myself.
In my arms, you see peace.

In our minds, we are now complete.
In our minds, our vision is reality.

Your humble servant,
Twilight

WORSHIPER

The word teaches that
God doesn't hear the prayer of sinners.

But the ones that worship God, and do His will,
those prayers he hears.

Who are you?

"Live in your Vision,
and you shall always be Happy!"

Your humble servant,
Twilight

EDUCATOR

It has been said,
the eyes are the windows to the soul,

but your eyes appear
to be the window to your mind.

Upon first look into your windows,
I saw overwhelming sadness.

I was unable to see the cause of your sadness.

Upon second look into your windows,
I saw great strength.

Hope! Hope of all the children
happy and fully engaged in the lesson.

Mostly, your great strength comes from your desire
of helping make this vision become reality.

Thank you for the second look.

Your humble servant,
Twilight

CAPTURED

I glimpsed in her eyes,
and was captured by that one glimpse.

That one glimpse gave me a glimmer of hope
for true love.

True, actual, and real,
I actually saw love in her eyes.
That love really touched my soul.

On this, the day of Our Lord,
I say thank you for the glimpse.

Your humble servant,
Twilight

Made in the USA
Columbia, SC
22 February 2023

12830096R00050